MONSTER POETRY

CUMBRIA

Edited By Megan Roberts

First published in Great Britain in 2018 by:

YoungWriters

Young Writers
Remus House
Coltsfoot Drive
Peterborough
PE2 9BF
Telephone: 01733 890066
Website: www.youngwriters.co.uk

FOREWORD

Young Writers was created in 1991 with the express purpose of promoting and encouraging creative writing. Each competition we create is tailored to the relevant age group, hopefully giving each child the inspiration and incentive to create their own piece of writing, whether it's a poem or a short story. We truly believe that seeing it in print gives pupils a sense of achievement and pride in their work and themselves.

Our latest competition, Monster Poetry, focuses on uncovering the different techniques used in poetry and encouraging pupils to explore new ways to write a poem. Using a mix of imagination, expression and poetic styles, this anthology is an impressive snapshot of the inventive, original and skilful writing of young people today. These poems showcase the creativity and talent of these budding new writers as they learn the skills of writing, and we hope you are as entertained by them as we are.

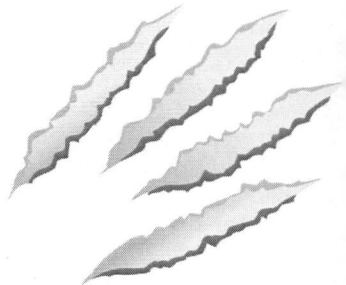

CONTENTS

Kirkby Stephen Primary School, Kirkby Stephen

Yvaine Braithwaite	59
Chloe Grace Murphy (9)	60
James Armer (9)	62
Holly Treece (9)	63
Harry Banks (9)	64
Marshall Repton (9)	65
Lucas noah Bousfield (9)	66
Lacey Metcalfe (9)	67
Harley Spooner (9)	68
Mollie Wealleans (8)	69
Louis Witterick (9)	70
Aliya Ella Mahata (9)	71
Sam Davis	72
Isabel Sansom (9)	73

Low Furness CE Primary School, Great Urswick

Mia Patricia Neild (9)	74
Isabelle W (8)	77
Daniel (9)	78
Kiki Lumb	81
Grace Alexandra Hartley (8)	82
Grace Low	84
Sam Sibley (8)	87
Euan Kelly (9)	88
Isla Robertson (9)	90
Katy Parsons	93
Ethan Harvey (9)	94
Lottie Mahony	96
Jack Manion (9)	98
Ben Hopkins (9)	100
Demi Elizabeth Garnett (9)	103
Kate C	104
Faith Leigh Rhodes	106
Frazier Brian Hazlehurst (9)	108
Phoebe Day (8)	110
Harvey Rhys Westwood (9)	112
Ruby Enfys Fountain (9)	114
Orla S (8)	116
Toby (9)	118

Florence Adams (8)	120
Rosie Lumb	121
Zach Parkinson (8)	122
Georgia Pip Sherrington (8)	123
Rohan Shaw	124
Theo	125
Grace Elizabeth Jewell (8)	126

North Lakes School, Penrith

Jake Carr (10)	127
Ruby Gordon (10)	128
Crystal McGuinness (10)	129
Jay Whear (9)	130
Gipsy Anne Scamp (10)	131
Eleonora Mitkus (10)	132
Oliver Lake (10)	133
Alexis McGuinness (11)	134
Simona Misiute (10)	135
Sam Ramsay (9)	136
Claudiu Perdei (10)	137
Mia Sedlak (9)	138
Kai Sowerby (10)	139
Byron Symes (10)	140
Darius Pelin (10)	141

North Walney Primary School, Walney Island

Jack Forsyth (9)	142
James McQuistan (9)	144
Freya Grace Thomas (7)	145
Amy Hunt (9)	146
Esme Hambleton (8)	147

Northside Primary School, Northside

Dakota Ayanna Fulton (8)	148

Ormsgill Nursery & Primary School, Barrow-In-Furness

Amy-Lee Summer Harris (9)	150
Keira Nelson (10)	151
Rya Bentley (11)	152
Keelan Lee Purcell (10)	153
Yazmin Martin (10)	154

St Thomas CE Primary School, Kendal

Jamie Swanton (8)	155
Thomas Perruzza (9)	156
Talitha Rushton (9)	158
Annabel Towler (9)	160
Molly-May Holleran (9)	162
Florrie Stalker (8)	164
Joseph William Green (8)	166
Norah Murray (8)	168
Layla Goodyear (9)	170
Caitlin Suzanne Whittaker (8)	172
Skye Atkinson (8)	174
Nicole Fiderewicz (9)	176
Chris Russel (9)	178
Seb Cox (8)	180
Amy Fiderewicz (9)	182
Keisha Miller (9)	184
Jackson Barber (9)	186
Jay Grattan (9)	188
Jenson Jay Hawad (8)	190
Aimee Louise Taylor (9)	191

THE POEMS

Ika Ika And Bungle

Ika Ika lives in the jungle
And has one friend, Bungle.
Ika Ika and Bungle roam across the land
And play instruments like a band.
They chase monkeys and put them in a pot,
Sometimes Ika Ika makes the pot too hot.
He looks a bit like a flower,
However, he doesn't have flower power.
Ika Ika lives in a box
And has a pet fox.
They swim in rivers and lakes,
But always leave whenever there's earthquakes.
Sometimes Bungle feels like he's out of the way,
But whenever he's upset, Ika Ika will ask to play.
Ika Ika's favourite food is monkey pies
And every time he gets one, with joy he cries.
As we wave goodbye to the fox,
Ika Ika and Bungle,
We wave goodbye to the jungle.

Cole Taylor (10)
Arlecdon Primary School, Arlecdon

About Jack Poem

My name is Jack,
I was born in a sack,
I am not a good monster,
I am a gangster!

I grew up in Crypton,
But I never knew Captain,
Captain Danazs,
Who made life crazy.

I am who I am,
I can't change that,
I am not a lamb,
But I am an infant just like Matt.

I once was bad,
But now I am good,
My mother was sad,
But now she has my hood.

My mum is lovely,
My mum is kind,

I may be a monster,
But I love her blind.

My family is great,
We all love our traits,
We may be mad,
But we're never sad.

Freddie Dear (9)
Arlecdon Primary School, Arlecdon

Goodbye My Life

I was once normal, living a normal life,
Until I saw a portal that took away my life.
I was worried, so I soon scuffled,
In a very big hurry.
The portal was closing,
So I jumped in while posing.
The world changed in a flash,
As I saw someone get whiplash.
Smack!
My head went *crack!*
I'm changing, my head is big,
My eyes are large,
I smell like marge,
There is a rocket barrage.

Deven Fowler (10)
Arlecdon Primary School, Arlecdon

Aly Fan

He is as big as five double-decker buses,
His eyes are as big as two trees,
His teeth are as sharp as a machete,
His body is as fat as two schools put together,
His feet are as long as two houses put together,
His arms are as long as Mr Fantastic's,
His claws are as sharp as a knife,
His eyes change colours eight times a second,
His neck is as fat as two cars on top of each other.

Bailey Jai Stevenson (10)
Arlecdon Primary School, Arlecdon

Blob All Alone

One mystical morning,
There was a shape-shifting fiend.
He had never ever met a human being.
The hairy fiend got out of his terrifying bed,
With an old, red bump on his furry head.

He had twelve tiny eyes which were a small size,
He was called Blob, never before
Had he had a surprise.
The ferocious, snarling beast
Went inside his lava cage,
His colour was a scary beige.
Blob said he never wanted friends to keep,
Because he never wanted them to beep.

Blob built a rocket one day,
He didn't even pay.
He flew to Blackpool, he really enjoyed it,
Everyone was surrounding him a bit.

Blob got really cross and sat angrily
On a full, grey rock.
It was a scary shock.

He cried out loud and never stopped,
He was very hot.

He flew back in his rocket,
With a shiny £2 coin in his pocket.
He didn't like his cousins,
Because they were always buzzing.

Blob didn't have much money,
But he really liked honey.
He lay down on his bed,
With his face all red,
Finally, he was all alone,
With his fancy, cuddly toy bone.
He was very happy,
But a little pappy,
"Thank you," he said
While lying in his bed.

Isla Johnston (9)
Boltons CE Primary School, Wigton

The Slithery Mystery

In the middle of the night,
Some people were given a fright
When something came
Slithering down the road,
Which looked nothing like a toad.
It had no legs and it had three heads,
It was as big as two sheds,
He was called Boog,
He was very rude.

He was very mean,
He was also very keen,
Unfortunately, he had no friends,
All he had were a few pens,
He could also count in tens.

He got in his rocket and, there in his pocket,
Was a smooth ten pound note.
He got out of the rocket and got in a boat,
He went past Big Ben,
Which, that year, was 110.

He got off the boat
And he looked at a goat.
Everybody ran off
And, with a bit of a cough,
He went to the rocket,
Still with the smooth ten pound note in his pocket,
He flew into the beautiful, blue sky
And then he ate a crispy pie
And he started to cry.

Boog got home
And, on top of his dome,
Was something like a sign,
That showed us all the time.
Boog walked into the house
And saw a little mouse,
But in his tiny room,
He listened to a tune
And he was very happy.
He ended the night
With no more frightened people.

Joseph Rumney (8)
Boltons CE Primary School, Wigton

My Monster Poem

After sunset in Egypt, a monster called Gooey
Lurked out from the petrifying pyramid's shadows.
She said bye to her shadow friends
And set off to Paris.
On the way, something changed inside her heart,
She learned to be polite, not rude.
When she got to Paris,
She started to explore and make friends.
But, once she saw the outside world,
She ran back to the underworld.

Three hours later, she ran
To her pretty dream home,
She met up with her old friend, Alex,
And they went to the Harris Cafe
And had some lovely beans on toast
And then went to see the snow-white ghost,
Then went for a ride on their boat.

When they got to the Eiffel Tower,
They tried to climb it.

It was taller so they thought it would never end,
But soon they got to the top
And had a bottle of Magic Pop.

Alex jumped onto Gooey's back,
Who jumped and landed not so flat,
They had a horse take them to the park.
As they played on the swings,
Everyone became interested in Gooey.
They played all day until it was time to go home,
Oh, what a shame.
So Alex and Gooey ran on home
And they all lived happily, ever after.

Lily Crosby (7)
Boltons CE Primary School, Wigton

Night Claw

At the beginning of midnight,
When the moon was out,
An enormous monster began to wake.
With fire in its eyes and great, big horns,
With razor-spinning feet and ten centimetre claws.
It was mean, it was evil,
And its name was Scarlet Claws.

She went into town to steal her tea,
But all she ate was money and bunnies,
So she took some coins and a rabbit's leg,
She ate them quickly so she was nearly dead.
At eleven o'clock in the morning,
As the monster was still snoring,
She slowly opened her eyes
And got a huge surprise.

It was another monster.
His name was Bobby Bobby Gobby,
As he had a giant gob.
They both sat down while wearing a crown,

Both of them made friends,
With good human blends.
They had the same horns and then they yawned,
They slept for days while snorting neighs,
But they were not horses.
They realised that they were brother and sister.

They each went home to watch some Rome,
Which was their favourite TV show.
They both were good and fell in the mud,
As Scarlet and Bobby got a good hobby
And lived a happy life.

Amber Gray (9)
Boltons CE Primary School, Wigton

Danger

Danger was a stranger,
To anyone who met him.
He was a mischief maker,
With tentacles, double two,
But his colour was an unusual blue.

He lived in a tin that looked like a bin,
Under the deep, blue sea.
He was a miniature Spockterpus,
With tentacles like an octopus
And was born on an island.

He had a magic key,
That was hidden in a tree,
It was spiky and gold,
But very hard to hold.
It was like an alligator's jaw,
Although it was a lot more.

He took the key and went to see
The cave of his father.
His father was a famous Spockterpus

And he had a disease called Tockerlus,
Therefore, he invented Tockertus.

His name was Professor Fiddlesticks,
He made a few tweeks and twizzles and ticks
And then he was done with his invention.

Danger really missed his dad,
Even though he was never bad.
He cried all day and he cried all night,
Then he realised he'd been a fright.
The next day, he apologised
And I thought he'd been hypnotised.

Keira Morrison (8)
Boltons CE Primary School, Wigton

My Monster Poem

At the Devil's hour, I heard a large thump,
And the rusty, old mansion shook.
My brother said, "Get Donald Trump."
I looked out of my slowly cracking window
At the dark, bumpy street
And saw what I thought were two tiny dots.
They didn't stop until they came off the road,
Into a pile of straw in a field.
My brother said, "Go down there if you dare."
He really did give me a scare, so I said, "Yeah."

I tiptoed silently down the stairs,
Towards the front door.
But, oops, I tripped and landed on the floor.
I didn't want to go,
But I went to the fence and stayed low,
I thought, *I have to go now and see this beast,*
He could have given me some armour at least.
I went over nervously,
I went over harmlessly,

The three-headed, disgusting monster
Was sitting under a tree,
Chances are, it wanted to be free.

Harvey-Lincoln Clark (9)

Boltons CE Primary School, Wigton

The Monster And The Kitty

At the end of the daylight,
A menacing monster awoke.
He smelled like a tree,
But who knew what he needed.
He liked to start chaos
And never liked to stop.

One day, he set off
In his small, black ship.
When he entered Planet Earth,
He started to feel a little sick.
But, when he began to land,
He found himself in New York City.
He wandered around for a little while,
But then found a tiny kitty.
He went up to the kitty and said, "Hello."
So, he took the kitty
And went to his fine home.

Ben Smith (9)
Boltons CE Primary School, Wigton

The Purple Blob

One black, gloomy, scary night,
A person saw a scary sight,
They saw a monster that had one eye
And it really did jump too high.
It was a shape like some jelly,
Although a bit too smelly.
It jumped in the rocket,
With some money in its pocket.
His rainbow eyes looked up and down,
His two spiky teeth giggled round and round,
He landed on his planet that he had abandoned
And there, he was so happy.
He played with his dear friends.
Sam was now a very happy monster,
All the others thought, indeed.

Lyla May Ewart (9)
Boltons CE Primary School, Wigton

Grizzles The Monster

One shadowy night,
He woke up to a terrible sight,
He uncovered his body
And went to the potty,
Even though he was still a bit noddy.
His eyes were blacker than ink
And his body was bright pink.
He went to the sink to have a drink,
Then he walked downstairs,
With a couple of pears.
He jumped on his bike
And called, "You sike!"
He saw a plane just above Spain
And said, "What a day it has been as a teen."
He arrived at his home sweet home
And went into his zone.

Ella Scott-Richardson (9)
Boltons CE Primary School, Wigton

My Monster Poem

After a little fright,
There was a monster,
Oh, what a scary sight!
The red-eyed demon was running to town
And laughing like a toad.
People ran away from the scary name,
Which wasn't even scary at all.
He was getting closer and closer and closer,
He was ready to shout out,
He really didn't doubt.
He ran away with a different name,
He pulled out a pitchfork and flew away,
He said, "I will scare you next time."
But he wasn't going to today.

Harvey Parker (7)
Boltons CE Primary School, Wigton

My Monster Stink Poem

In the morning, what a terrible morning,
Stink got up and started yawning.
He could hear the big drops pouring,
On his big, extreme cave.
He went to bathe in his famous bath
And also walk his dog along the path.
As he walked with his dog,
He jumped as he thought he saw a frog,
But it was not what he thought.
In fact, it was a strange green blob,
Which grew bigger with every drop of rain.
Stink stood back and watched it grow,
Until it turned into a monster toad!

Lucy Smith (9)
Boltons CE Primary School, Wigton

The Monster Called Mars Bar

When I went into the galaxy,
I had just passed Mercury,
I saw a tiny, sweet and beautiful thing
On a planet. When I landed,
I asked, "What's your name?"
"I'm Mars-Bar," replied the monster.
"All my friends call me the Pongster."
"Do you have a teacher?" I asked.
"Yes, her name is Mrs Dennison," replied Mars-Bar.
"Mrs Dennison is very nice,
She plays with dice."
"Goodbye for now, I will miss you so,"
I whispered with a tear in my eye.
"I'll visit your planet soon," Mars-Bar shouted.
"I'll cause lots of mischief,"
Mars-Bar said to himself.
I didn't trust Mars-Bar any more.

Millie Pratt (9)
Derwent Vale Primary School, Great Clifton

The Wave

The Wave was created in a tsunami,
Lots of adventures came crashing down.
It wasn't The Wave, it was a tsunami!

It whirled me in,
I tried to swim out,
But I woke up in the Arctic,
Little paws were tapping my face.
It was The Wave.

We knew we were going to be friends,
I asked, "Would you like to go on an adventure?"
Because The Wave loves adventures,
She nodded with her fuzzy head.

She was only thirty centimetres,
But she was very strong.
We travelled around the Arctic.
We heard the crashing waves,
We tasted the cold, winter air.
Then she took me home.

A few weeks passed,
She said she would be back today.
But at the door, I saw a monster,
With fiery skin and yellow eyes...

Aisha Sanderson (8)
Derwent Vale Primary School, Great Clifton

The Story Of The Carl Floss

I was born in a haunted house.
My mother and father were giant ink monsters,
I was a haunted monster.

I had no friends because I was evil,
We didn't have next door neighbours,
I was bad-tempered and I was vicious.

I went on holiday, I was in a volcano.
Soon after, we were on Planet Earth.
We saw humans and
They were running away from my family.

I heard people sing at the church,
They were running away from me,
I smelled blood and it smelled delicious.
I fell to the ground and they ran away,
Because I was getting up.

I tasted ice cream, it was disgusting,
I tasted it on the beach.
I ran and ran, until I found a huge house

And I went in and got some clothes
And danced around.

Owen Opie (8)

Derwent Vale Primary School, Great Clifton

Ovencago's Adventure

Ovencago Buzz lives in Gigmilgour
With her friends.
She really loves it there.
Ovencago Buzz went on an adventure,
To Bubble Gum Land.

She was still flying,
When a Moncayo bird came.
It was ravenous.
The huge bird had two, enormous eyes,
With a great, blue beak
And orange feathers.

Ovencago arrived in Bubble Gum Land,
But, there was a strange thing.
Ovencago felt weird,
Like she had a mixed feeling.

The bird felt cheerful,
The bird felt famished,
He opened his huge beak
And gobbled Ovencago.

Was it the very end?
The bird died
Because Ovencago had
Toxic, hirsute fur.
Ovencago went home,
Everyone in Gigmilgour was thrilled.

Hannah Chapman-Arts (10)
Derwent Vale Primary School, Great Clifton

Monsters In Thin Air?

It was a cold, dark night,
I was on my own, at home,
My mam and dad were on a date,
I was downstairs, watching TV.
All of a sudden, the door squeaked open.
"It wasn't time for them to come back yet,"
I whispered to myself.
I peered through the crack of the door,
It was monsters!

I dashed to find a hiding spot,
At last I found one,
It was hard because my house is only tiny.
Then they sneaked in slowly with each small step.
All of a sudden,
They morphed into my parents!
Then they found me,
Would it be the end?

But it was my real mam and dad,
With a piece of cake for looking after the house.
But what happened to the third monster...?

Dayne Kenneth Gallacher (10)
Derwent Vale Primary School, Great Clifton

The Lonely Little Monster

On a chilly but warm morning,
I was wandering to school,
When I saw something that blew my mind.
It was a monster,
A lonely, little monster.
He said he was concerned,
He said he was lost,
I said I would help him find his way.
"I have to pay," I heard him say,
So I buckled down and paid for him.
He was fizzy and dizzy when I held his hand,
But I just laughed and said it tickled.
"You're very friendly for a monster," I said
And he left and yelled that he'd visit.
And yes, he was rejected and fluffy,
But he was one big cotton head.

Louisa Draper (8)
Derwent Vale Primary School, Great Clifton

Me And My Monster

Me and my monster go on adventures,
Exciting adventures.
My monster is called Papyrus,
It is only kind to me.
My monster is from the Dark Planet,
My monster has friends on Dark Planet.
It is cuddly in its heart.
My monster is only 210 millimetres tall,
But it is very scary.
You will never see it,
It is too timid.
I found it when people
Were cruelly kicking it,
So I shouted, "Go away!"
They ran like headless chickens,
To America and far away
And together, my monster and I
Never had to say goodbye.

Shaun Taylor (8)
Derwent Vale Primary School, Great Clifton

My Monster Adventures

My monster came from Planet Zork,
He did have friends, but not with him,
He was bad, I made sure he was not,
This was how I met him.

My job was an astronaut,
I soared across the stars,
I was in a micro-ship,
It was very risky using a micro-ship.
I was exploring new planets,
An immensely big monster had broken its legs
And I took care of it.

The micro-ship suddenly fell,
I tried to pull up,
But the handle snapped.
The monster breathed fire
Into the fuel system
And we landed safely.

Charlie Breen (9)
Derwent Vale Primary School, Great Clifton

Believer's Dreams

This poem starts at Malata Fort,
Where the danger happens.
I was on my own at Malata Fort.
It was scary because
The clock tower was falling down.
There was Believer sleepwalking,
So I went to see what was wrong.

I jumped out the window like a monkey,
I was scared something was wrong,
So I checked his cogs. Then I found a syringe
And, on the label, it said, 'Go to sleep poison'.
I pulled it out and then we went home.
That's when Mam and Dad came home
And we were in so much trouble...

Fletcher King (8)
Derwent Vale Primary School, Great Clifton

My Friend Grunt

I first met Grunt at school,
He was fuzzy and blue,
My friends screamed,
I stayed and said hello.
A grown man screamed,
For, on his back, lay a roach,
Snoring away.
And, from that day forth,
We were friends.

It was lunch,
Grunt smelled sausages sizzling
So he went to the kitchen,
Where it was cooling.
He saw the cook drooling,
He snatched a sausage with his tusks
And was kicked out.
So, he flew off.

I hope he visits again,
He said he will.

Laiton William Sharpe (10)
Derwent Vale Primary School, Great Clifton

The Brownie Eater

On my holiday, I found a monster called Brownie,
She is very fluffy and brown.
She's not a lost pet at all,
She lives with Dad, Mum, and Baby Brother.
Right now, she is really friendly.
Not long after, we became good friends.
We smelled the ice cream
Coming from the ice cream van,
We felt the water as we swam in the pool,
We played in the park and on the swings
And we climbed up mountains.
I hope Brownie will play again, she said she will.

Abi-Leigh Burgess (10)
Derwent Vale Primary School, Great Clifton

Maltesers

On my way to school one day,
There was a monster who wanted to play,
So I said, "What's your name?"
He shouted, "Malteser, now what's yours then?"
The monster was shaggy, he looked like a hen.
So I replied, "Connor, now what've you done?"
Malteser was dejected, so I said, "Are you hurt?"
But he was actually being strict!
"Come and see me again soon,
When I visit the Moon!"

Connor McAvoy (9)
Derwent Vale Primary School, Great Clifton

The Killer!

The Killer was born in Death Forest,
He had bloody teeth and slimy scales.
Alone and lonely, he wandered
Through the deep, dark wood,
Hunting for innocent deer,
Imagining its sweet, raw taste,
In his immense, toxic mouth.
Then he entered a deep, dark cave,
Looking for its prey,
For the next day.
Until I made him pay.
I set up a trap one fine day
And he fell for it and I screamed, "Hooray!"

Jamie Michael Black (10)
Derwent Vale Primary School, Great Clifton

The Monster Called Blob

I brought my red, hirsute ball,
It bounced and rolled.
It was a ball with legs,
Jumping and rolling in anger,
Craziness all around.
At the pool, everyone ran in fear
Everyone but me.
I took the monster by its arms and shouted,
"Blob! Blob! Blob!"
As it bounced off the walls,
Blob started to fade away.
My heart was broken,
My friend was gone,
That night, I cried myself to sleep.

Elise Kirby High (10)
Derwent Vale Primary School, Great Clifton

Serpent

One stormy day, the Sea Serpent came.
He may have no friends,
Because he's not the same.
He also ate fish in a large dish,
He slept on the ocean floor,
Like a human in their bed.
All he wanted was a friend
To spend the weekend with,
Until he met me.
I heard his call from the waterfall,
So I went to check.
I searched for hours and hours and hours,
But nothing.

Cole Ashton Burgess (10)
Derwent Vale Primary School, Great Clifton

It's Adventure

It was made out of toxic waste,
Toxi drank toxic waste,
Because he couldn't drink water.
It made people feel unpleasant and obnoxious,
It smelled like poisonous acid.
After a while, he left his home place,
And went to go on an adventure.
He met me at the beach,
He was burning because of the water,
He was like an ice cream melting.
I saved the whole world...

Caitlin Addison (9)
Derwent Vale Primary School, Great Clifton

Back In Time With My Pet Monster

One day, I was in history class,
I met a vicious monster,
We went back in time,
To see the Vikings.
My monster was called Mr Lusy.
We got to fight the Saxons.
I trained Mr Lusy,
But I couldn't see his face,
He was hirsute.
Finally, we ate a banquet.
In the end, he was joyful,
Fuzzy and bushy.
Funny, I have a teacher called Mr Lucy...

Katie Hall (9)
Derwent Vale Primary School, Great Clifton

The Candy Monster

When I went to a galaxy,
I found a pink palaxy.
It was made of sugar and candy,
There was a cute, stylish creature
Called Cotton Floss
And loved to eat candy.
She was the colour of pops,
She was my friend!
I shouted, "Bye, bye!"
In the palaxy of candy canes.
"We'll meet again!" I shouted with glee.

Kaitlyn Riley (9)
Derwent Vale Primary School, Great Clifton

Big Bad Buster...

When I went to space,
There was a big place,
There was a hirsute monster
And was also a bogster.
He looked dejected
Because he had no friends,
He looked possessed
Because of his master,
Because he looked just like pasta.
His master called him grotesque
Because he was miniscule.

Lorton Curnow (9)
Derwent Vale Primary School, Great Clifton

The Crazy Monster

On my way to the beach,
I saw a giant monster.
He ran until he found a house,
I ran in and he was there!
He was six foot two.
Then he went upstairs
And got some clothes,
Then danced around the room
And then ran away.

Alexia May Cargo (8)
Derwent Vale Primary School, Great Clifton

The Flopp

The lizard moves at his own speed,
Quick, slow, whatever he needs.
He is as purple as a grape,
He walks on two legs,
With a lizard-like shape.
His spikes are pointy like a knife,
He says he lives a peaceful life,
His name is Floop, he is a flopp.
He loves fishing and cannot stop.
He speaks roughly, but I have to say,
He is quite friendly, trust me!

He lives in a cave, near a river,
He has a snake friend who can slither.
Her name is Night, she loves to fight,
Her arms turn into snakes, and she likes cakes.
His name is Floop, he is a flopp,
He loves to make friends down by the dock.

Dawn Borradaile (10)
Gillford Centre, Carlisle

Slime Shady

Slime Shady, with his googly eyes and acid smile,
Sat on the planet Jupiter all the time.
Today, his planet was attacked
By millions of naughty aliens,
But Slime Shady bit back with his sharp fangs
And he killed some aliens!
Slime Shady was turning vicious,
As the blood from the aliens was not nutritious.
As vicious as a tiger,
Slime Shady put some slime on his feet
And slipped on his rocket boots.
With a hoot and a toot, Slime Shady disappeared.
Slime Shady found a purple portal,
Which whizzed him off to a new life in the jungle.

Frankie Hodgson (8)
Gillford Centre, Carlisle

Slithering Snake

Deep in the dungeon of the castle,
Lives a scary, monster-sized snake.
Tiptoe quietly in case he wakes,
His skin is as black as night,
His green eye glimmers in the light,
Make sure you don't speak,
Or you will hear his haunting hiss.
If you think you can escape,
You will need to be fast,
His tongue is long and it sure won't miss.
Keep in the shadows for there is also
A grand wizard who is friends with the snake.

Owen Welsh Graham (11)
Gillford Centre, Carlisle

Thing Of A King

Slouching, grouching, always watching,
Mooching, looking, always snooping,
Why, oh why must you do what you do?
Why, oh why must you steal all our things?
Why, oh why must you steal all our drink?
Why, oh why must you steal our clothes?
Why, oh why Mr Thing?
Why, oh why must you do what you do?

Jamie Peter Gray
Gillford Centre, Carlisle

My Monster At The Cinema

I met the hairy creature at the cinema
And he was as hairy as a bear
And as cute as a puppy
And as scary as a messy bear.
I said, "What are you and what are you doing here?"
The monster said, "I am from Planet Zog
And I ran away because
My family was being mean to me."
I said, "Do you want
To come to my house after the film?"
The monster said okay.

The film finished,
Me and Fearful the monster
Went to my house
And had some tea and a drink.
Then it was time for Fearful to go home.
I hope he would come again next time!

Carys Abigayle Lowe (8)
Goodly Dale Primary School, Windermere

When I Made Friends With A Monster

I heard some footsteps,
Some great, big footsteps.
I saw a shadow.
I looked up and there was
A big, bad, blue monster.
I ran and ran, the monster said,
"Stop! I come in pieces!"
I thought he meant peace.
I stopped and he said, "I want a friend."
I said I would be his friend.
We went to my house and,
When we got there,
My mum and dad
Were screaming and shouting.
I said it was okay.
We had a great time together,
Sadly, he had to go.
I said, "Will you come again?"
"Yes," he said.

Alex Milligan (9)
Goodly Dale Primary School, Windermere

Robbery

One night, I met a monster,
It was three o'clock and I shrieked.
He looked creepy, deadly and sharp.
He said, "Can we be friends?"
I wanted to go for a robbery.
When we got outside, he said, "Let's go,"
And we headed to the bank.

We stopped and said, "Let's go."
When we got outside,
We went back to his house.
I put the money under his bed.
I said, "I have to go."
"Boy," he said. "Boy, come back tomorrow."

Honzik Stecher (8)
Goodly Dale Primary School, Windermere

When We Had Tea With The Queen

I met this funny monster at the funfair yesterday.
I said, "Do you want the meet the queen
And have tea and come and play?"
He said," Yes!"
And then, for a minute, I was scared,
But he was as cute as a soggy dog.
He was as happy as a hippo,
And as hairy as a bear.
I asked him, "Do you have a friend?"
He said, "Yes."
So we went to go and meet the queen,
And have a cup of tea.
I can't wait until the next time
He comes to visit me.

Paige Parkinson-Chapman (8)
Goodly Dale Primary School, Windermere

The Day I Was On Another Planet

I was in my garden when I met a monster,
She was like a shining diamond.
She never spoke, but she took me
On a journey to her planet,
Her planet was as shiny as a crystal.
I swam in her swimming pool,
I tasted her cake, it was as sweet as sugar
And we watched the glitter birds
High in the sky, dancing on the breeze.
But, when the sun came down,
The monster turned to glitter.
I was alone and all the next day,
I wondered if it was just a dream.

Felicity Pattinson (8)
Goodly Dale Primary School, Windermere

When My Monster Came To School

One day, I was in my garden
When a monster appeared from space.
He told me that he was a shape-shifter
And he was cheeky and super sneaky
And his name was Toffee.

I took him to school one day.
At break time, he broke everything in his way,
And at lunch time, he ate all the food.
He spied on the teachers' meeting every afternoon.
The teachers were as suspicious as a detective,
But they never found out!

Pablo Nunez De Castro (8)
Goodly Dale Primary School, Windermere

Giggles The Monster

Once, I was going to school,
When I saw a purple and pink monster thing.
It looked cute, happy and fluffy,
It was playing.

Then it saw me and came down,
She was friendly.
Then we, in some way, became friends.
We went into school
And I changed my shoes
And into class we went.

She went in there and made new friends.
We had fun and played with friends,
But then it was time for her to go.

Iarina Stefania Miron (8)
Goodly Dale Primary School, Windermere

The Boss

The Boss and his team were evil and mean,
They came from outer space.
They landed on Earth in a dark, gloomy cave,
And plotted to destroy the Earth.
I followed a meteor into the cave.
It was gloomy, apart from their headlight eyes.
It smelled like bacon and I was nervous,
In the dark, I had a surprise.
They looked at me and chased me,
I ran and ran until I got tired,
And hid behind a bin!

Henley Randall (8)
Goodly Dale Primary School, Windermere

Horns

One day, an egg came from a volcano.
Bang! The egg cracked.
A little monster came out near an erupting volcano.
It was on the news and I went to the volcano.
He was standing on top of the volcano.
His colour was gloomy yellow
And he had yellow eyes,
He was surrounded by fire.
It was the Drogon, the dangerous shape-shifter.

Tyler Skarratt (9)
Goodly Dale Primary School, Windermere

Britney Spears

I wake up in the morning, just to see
A great, big monster that looks like me.
We go to Walby Farm Park to have a bit of fun,
We go down the bumpy slide
And have a bit of a run.
I look around and see she's gone,
I go around and look for her and then I see a
sheep.
There's a cupboard I shouldn't look in,
But I think I'll take a peek.
I see a whole new world with a burgundy slide,
I think I might just go and have a ride.
Then I hear a bang and a clash,
I wonder what it is, and just then,
She pops out and runs straight back in.
I think that I might just go and play some more
So, if you don't move your butt right now,
I'm going to get poor.
So no more treats for you my friend,
Until you're nearly four.

Yvaine Braithwaite
Kirkby Stephen Primary School, Kirkby Stephen

Fuzzy's Adventure

One morning, it was pouring.
But the queen didn't care,
For she strolled to the beach
For a paddle.

But, when she got to the beach,
The sun was shimmering, shining
Like a million diamonds
From a jewellery store!

In a shamrock bush was
A fuzzy, legless
And small monster.
He was green with a unibrow.

They jumped on the sun beds,
The monster mentioned that his name was Fuzzy.
The queen asked where he came from.
Fuzzy said, "From a hairdresser's."

In a bag of hair,
He could not bear to see himself.

But he was quite surprised,
He liked it.

The queen lay on a lilo,
Fuzzy sat on top of her,
She didn't mind,
Because she was really kind.

Chloe Grace Murphy (9)
Kirkby Stephen Primary School, Kirkby Stephen

Bob

I was on the loo,
When I met a blue monster,
He was six foot two.
At half past two,
I jumped off the red loo.
The monster said,
"Should we do some mischief?"
I said yes.
"Let's turn all the teddies
Into evil teddy bears."
I asked how he could do that.
He said, "I have magic."
I asked if we could save the day,
But that sounded boring,
So we set off.

Ten years later, we had the last teddy.
You might wonder,
Why it took us so long,
But some people had more than one.

James Armer (9)
Kirkby Stephen Primary School, Kirkby Stephen

Me And My Monster

This special monster was born in a tornado,
Where she lives, there's lots of bitter cocoa.
Behind a twisty willow tree,
Tiera the rosy red, scaly monster met me.
We twirled around the slippy slope,
Then we climbed up lots of thick rope.
We liked to spend time together
And make special, sticky monster cakes
And visit blue lakes.
We danced under the moon,
To a very jazzy tune.
She sang on her karaoke machine,
Her favourite dance is the hokey-cokey.
Tiera lives under my bed,
But sometimes, she bumps her head.

Holly Treece (9)
Kirkby Stephen Primary School, Kirkby Stephen

Victor, The Ugly

When I woke up in the morning,
On the wall was a warning.
There was an ugly monster in the room,
Over by the window, he stood in the gloom.

I asked him, "Shall we go
To the beach for a row?"
He replied back, "Yes!
Yay! Let's go and get dressed!"

So off we went to the beach,
Where we ate a juicy peach.
We set up the tent,
But, unfortunately, it was bent.
Next, we went to bed,
Where we ate some home-made bread.

Harry Banks (9)
Kirkby Stephen Primary School, Kirkby Stephen

Zog

Zog was running through the street,
Covering his head was a bedsheet,
So I went to pick him up
And put him in a huge cup.
But sadly, when I got home,
Mum thought he was a gnome,
She put tea in the cup,
Which made him act up.

Having fallen in the cup, he began to steam,
All I could hear was his blood-curdling scream,
So I told my mum to stop.
Luckily it stopped being hot,
So me and Zog went to the shop.

Marshall Repton (9)

Kirkby Stephen Primary School, Kirkby Stephen

Fuz Fuz Fallout

One day, a monster called Fuz Fuz played away,
A rustle in the mammoth, green bushes,
Made Fuz Fuz trip on hay.

Fuz Fuz got up in a huff,
Tim pushed Fuz Fuz to keep him at bay,
Tim said lots of stuff,
Fuz Fuz said, "It's a nice, sunny day."

Fuz Fuz played on the swings all day,
Tim jogged away,
Fuz Fuz just wanted to play,
Tim still would not stay.

Lucas noah Bousfield (9)
Kirkby Stephen Primary School, Kirkby Stephen

Cuddles

Cuddles is my monster,
I made her up last week,
A monster so fluffy,
I cuddle her in my sleep.

Cuddles is my favourite monster,
Who likes to play games.
She has friends and
She likes making up their names.

When Cuddles goes out to play,
Lots of people shout, "Hooray!"
She may not look like an ordinary monster,
But she can also save the day!

Lacey Metcalfe (9)
Kirkby Stephen Primary School, Kirkby Stephen

Gobble Wobble's Story

In monster school,
There was a big-mouthed,
Purple, mischievous fuzzball
Called Gobble Wobble.
He loved to eat
And had no feet
And only two tails, of course.
Make him giggle,
Make him laugh,
That's what Gobble Wobble's all about!

Gobble Wobble, Gobble Wobble,
Was expelled from school,
For eating all the tables
And being a fool!

Harley Spooner (9)
Kirkby Stephen Primary School, Kirkby Stephen

Nosor

Nosor is a Spanish monster,
Who likes to eat lobster,
He goes to school,
But is wickedly cruel.

He's extremely fat,
He sits on a mat,
He eats all day long,
Also, he plays Spanish ping pong.

He is shockingly disgusting,
But very trusting,
When it comes to Spanish,
Nosor has to be banished.

Mollie Wealleans (8)
Kirkby Stephen Primary School, Kirkby Stephen

Fang

Fang has twenty-four navy eyes.
When he arrives,
It's always a surprise,
He teleports in and out,
It is horrible when he shouts.
Fang is invisible
And he loves to hide,
He is a good friend,
But he doesn't have a girlfriend.

Louis Witterick (9)
Kirkby Stephen Primary School, Kirkby Stephen

Aphmay

She saves herself from drowning,
She lives in Starlight Wonderland,
Her name is Aphmay.
She is amazingly honest,
Her skin is sparkly purple
And her clothes are multi-coloured.
Her hair is like a rainbow,
She is cute and mini.

Aliya Ella Mahata (9)
Kirkby Stephen Primary School, Kirkby Stephen

Monster In New York

He is taking over New York,
He lives on the 126th storey,
He's a business-monster in disguise.
He is extremely villainous,
He is shadowy and metal-coloured,
He is Zandorf the Great.

Sam Davis
Kirkby Stephen Primary School, Kirkby Stephen

Adele

A dventures are scary,

D aring rides,

E nemies are hairy,

L ovely hides,

E xhausting for a fairy.

Isabel Sansom (9)

Kirkby Stephen Primary School, Kirkby Stephen

Fear

On a dark and stormy night,
You'll be sure to get a fright,
When Fear comes out to play,
To come and make you pay.

The house that Fear lived in
Isn't there anymore,
But I'll tell you this my child,
The story will not make you snore.

On a dark and stormy night,
You'll be sure to get a fright,
When Fear comes out to play,
To come and make you pay.

Many years ago,
On this very night,
Fear was brought to this town,
By his parents in delight.

On a dark and stormy night,
You'll be sure to get a fright,

When Fear comes out to play,
To come and make you pay.

One day when Fear was asleep,
He was awoken by a loud clang.
"Be quiet," he said in a miserable grunt,
But then there was an even louder bang.

On a dark and stormy night,
You'll be sure to get a fright,
When Fear comes out to play,
To come and make you pay.

So he got out of bed
And went to the window
And saw a sign that said for sale,
Now this could be a show.

On a dark and stormy night,
You'll be sure to get a fright,
When Fear comes out to play,
To come and make you pay.

Then he knew what to do,
He didn't want the house to go,

So he thought of a plan,
To put on a scary show.

On a dark and stormy night,
You'll be sure to get a fright,
When Fear comes out to play,
To come and make you pay.

When the people came,
To look at his home,
Fear came out
And they all gave a groan.

On a dark and stormy night,
You won't get a fright,
Because Fear is happy now,
So you'll be safe, for now.

Mia Patricia Neild (9)

Low Furness CE Primary School, Great Urswick

Cheeky Meeky

Cheeky Meeky lives in a volcano
With fire and water.
She has two sisters called Meep and PF .
She sings like a popstar and is as kind as a human.
She left her family because it was too difficult,
They didn't have enough food.
One day Cheeky sneaked out at night.
She found Meep and said,
"Hi, I can't find PF let's go find her."
They set off on their adventure under the water,
They needed to find one sister.
They found PF singing under the coral.
Cheeky said, "Can I stay with you?" PF said, "Yes."
Cheeky Meeky unpacked her cases.
Cheeky did a cannon ball and made electricity.
Cheeky didn't know she could do that.

Isabelle W (8)
Low Furness CE Primary School, Great Urswick

Flame

On a nice summer day,
Flame came to play,
To make everybody pay,
On that hot summer day.

When did it come? Nobody knows,
Where did it come from? Nobody knows,
What's it's name? nobody knows,
How hot can it be? nobody knows,

As deadly as a shark,
100,000 degrees hot,
As fast as a cheetah.

On a nice summer day,
Flame came to play,
To make everybody pay,
On that hot summer day.

As hot as the sun,
As quiet as a mouse,
As mean as a lion,
As bright as the sun.

On a nice summer day,
Flame came to play,
To make everybody pay,
On that hot summer day.

When people come around his house,
He mite give you a bite,
You'll probably get a fright,
He might pinch you in the shadows of the night.

On a nice summer day,
Flame came to play,
To make everybody pay,
On that hot summer day.

If you wanted him to be nice you'll never be right,
You'll never want to wake him up at night,
He might eat you when you're in bed
And you might be right,
He might sneak in your bedroom when it's bright,

On a nice summer day,
Flame came to play to make,

To make everybody pay,
On that hot summer day.

If you push him in the water, he might be very light,
He might not be so mean, so go and check it out,
He could go in an aquarium if you were sure,
Somebody chucked him in the water
And was nice to everyone.

On a nice summer day,
Flame came to play
And was nice to everyone,
On that hot summer day.

Daniel (9)

Low Furness CE Primary School, Great Urswick

Meep

Meep lives in some seaweed and some coral.
She likes to count shells and also have some fun,
She has hands like tentacles and a scaly tail.
She is kooky and crazy with blue toenails.
She left her home on an adventure,
When she set off she felt like
It was getting later and later.
She carried on and she heard a scream,
It was just Riley, a giant,
With a thorn in one of his feet.
Meep pulled it out and he said, "Thanks"
And "What can I do for you?"
I said "Maybe a ride!"
He piked me up with his hands.
"Here you are in London," he said.
"See you next time!"

Kiki Lumb
Low Furness CE Primary School, Great Urswick

The Unlucky Mermaid

Pearl Fountain came from the mystical heavens
up above.
She has sickly green skin and a scaly tail,
She lives in the colourful coral reef,
She is kind and helpful and teaches goodness.
One day, PF was swimming in the coral when
Someone or something caught her hair.
She was dragged into a creepy cave.
Now that's how PF's adventure begins.

In the creepy cave, PF could just see
A green glowing figure.
PF froze.
She knew what this was:
An enemy to mermaid kind,
Her father called it the Inky Black Fiend.
PF gathered her courage and spoke,
"Who are you?"
"Shut up or I'll zap you!" screamed the Fiend.
"I'll zap you!" So she grabbed the zapper
And he melted to the ground!
Then he was gone.

She was on her way to the palace
When she was surrounded by
The Inky Black Fiends!
"We were watching you!" cackled one.
"You didn't know what that zapper did!"
"It created more of us!"
"Now you're on your own"
"And there are more than 9,600 of us!"
Screeched all of them at once.
"Then why was he
About to zap me?" asked PF angrily.
"So we would have more
Of you to eat!" they answered.
She could not take it. She had to give up.
And she did.

Grace Alexandra Hartley (8)
Low Furness CE Primary School, Great Urswick

Bop And The Cop

Bop, Bop was bouncing to the shop,
To buy some cupcakes,
But not a washing mop.
He was

Friendly, funny, fluffy,
Bouncy, boingy, bubbly,
Cute, cuddly, candy,
Dancey, dreamy, dandy.

Bop, Bop was bouncing to the shop,
To buy some jelly,
When he bumped into a cop.
He's not

Friendly, funny, fluffy,
Bouncy, boingy, bubbly,
Cute, cuddly, candy,
Dancey, dreamy, dandy.

Bop, Bop was bouncing to the shop,
To buy some ice cream,

When he said to the cop:
You're not

Friendly, funny, fluffy,
Bouncy, boingy, bubbly,
Cute, cuddly, candy,
Dancey, dreamy, dandy.

Bop, Bop was bouncing to the shop,
To buy some cherries,
When he saw the cop walk off.
He is

Friendly, funny, fluffy,
Bouncy, boingy, bubbly,
Cute, cuddly, candy,
Dancey, dreamy, dandy.

Bop, Bop was bouncing to the shop,
To buy some cupcakes,
But not a washing mop.
He was

Friendly, funny, fluffy,
Bouncy, boingy, bubbly,

Cute, cuddly, candy,
Dancey, dreamy, dandy.

Grace Low

Low Furness CE Primary School, Great Urswick

Monster Poem

He was born on Planet Zog.
It was a dark place, really, I mean bad place.
In that time it was a very dangerous place:
Newborn babies were slaves,
They were slaves for their whole life,
But soon, that would change.
Meet David, he is a newborn baby,
They saved him from the slaves.
He's the boy who's going to stop it!

Here's David again, he is older now.
He wants to change the world
And he actually does.
He meets up with me, Walliams.
They get ready for the plan!
They strike this evening.
They grab some babies and keep on going,
'Til they are all saved.
They have a party.

Sam Sibley (8)
Low Furness CE Primary School, Great Urswick

Rage's Tale

As slow as a snail,
As squidgy as slime,
As tall as Big Ben,
His favourite number is nine.

In a country far far away,
In a huge volcano,
Where nobody went to play,
Monsters lived.

In the volcano lived a monster named Rage,
He lived in this strange lava house,
With his awful Aunt Page
And lots of robots with the same name.

In a country far far away,
In a huge volcano,
Where nobody went to play,
Monsters lived.

Aunt Page tortured Rage every day,
Torture happened everywhere he went,

So Rage thought of a major plan to get away,
Even if it was risk to him and Aunt Page.

In a country far far away,
In a huge volcano,
Where nobody went to play,
Monsters lived.

Then came the day Rage's plan
Was going to strike,
So Rage pressed the button
And spikes came firing down.
Aunt Page died and the robots exploded,
Then the word spread all over town.

In a country far far away,
In a huge volcano,
Where nobody went to play,
Monsters lived.

Euan Kelly (9)
Low Furness CE Primary School, Great Urswick

Spiky Spoo

There is a little monster,
His name is Spiky Spoo,
One day he bought a cow,
That keeps on going moo.

Where does he live?
What does he do?
Is he good or bad?
He's Spiky Spoo!

Although he was a monster,
He took her everywhere,
To the shop, to the hairdresser's,
Even to the fair.

Where does he live?
What does he do?
Is he good or bad?
He's Spiky Spoo!

Spiky Spoo is up to no-good,
Tormenting Mrs Fig,

Tripping her up
And stealing her pig.

Where does he live?
What does he do?
Is he good or bad?
He's Spiky Spoo!

Mrs Fig doesn't like it,
"Stop it," she said.
Spiky Spoo dropped the pig
And then away he fled.

Where does he live?
What does he do?
Is he good or bad?
He's Spiky Spoo.

Spiky Spoo is happy now,
Because he has turned good,
He's dancing all around,
Celebrating with a pud.

Where does he live?
What does he do?

Is he good or bad?
He's Spiky Spoo!

Isla Robertson (9)
Low Furness CE Primary School, Great Urswick

The Ghost Cat

Solly was born in the high blue sky.
She looks like a ghost cat,
With long, long whiskers,
Smelling like a blueberry.
Solly was very silly.
Her friend would call her Silly Solly.
For a long time she wanted a friend,
But to get a friend she had to be kind.
She didn't know how to be kind.
One day she met a bubble moster,
His name was Bubble Bob.
"How are you so kind?" asked Solly.
"Well my advice is to practise," he said.
She practised by giving some juce!
"Well done," he said.
"Now offer a seat," he said.
She tried and tried,
Then she did it.
She was finally kind!

Katy Parsons
Low Furness CE Primary School, Great Urswick

The Life-Changing Walk

Vicious Vic is from outer space,
Has no friends and
Has one pale blue face.

Early in the morning,
On one sunny day,
He went for a walk
And saw a red cave.
He went on walking and
Saw a spider squawking.

Teeth like stubby crayons
And yellow like the sun.
He ate a big fish and
Said it was yum.
He smells of rotten fish,
Like his favourite dish.

Vicious Vic went in the red cave
And found Mr Sillyson lying in a grave,
He went on walking and
Saw a guy called Mace,
He punched him square in the face.

He went on walking,
Right past Mace and
Saw a naughty, dog-looking teacher,
Who looked like some sort of creature.

He was as colourful as Vic and
Liked to chase a stick,
He had a pet shark
And lost his bark.

They lived with each other,
In the same house,
They were best friends forever,
With a big scuttling mouse.

Ethan Harvey (9)
Low Furness CE Primary School, Great Urswick

Lily Cuddle-Paw

Lily Cuddle-Paw
Never wants some more,
She's cute, she's kind and ever so clever,
She'll be the best monster for ever!

Lily Cuddle-Paw
Is so good,
She'll never break the law,
But she does like a chocolate pud!

Lily Cuddle-Paw
Never wants some more,
She's cute, she's kind and ever so clever,
She'll be the best monster for ever!

Lily Cuddle-Paw
Is off to the store,
To buy some apples,
But not the core.

Lily Cuddle-Paw
Never wants some more,

She's cute, she's kind and ever so clever,
She'll be the best monster forever!

Lily Cuddle-Paw
Is the best at her school,
She writes lots of stories
And she's never a fool.

Lily Cuddle-Paw
Never wants some more,
She's cute, she's kind and ever so clever,
She'll be the best monster forever!

Lottie Mahony
Low Furness CE Primary School, Great Urswick

Tangle Foot

Sharp teeth to eat,
He hunts for food,
If he doesn't get it,
He goes in a mood.

His name is Tangle Foot,
He lives in a bog,
Would you like to meet him?
Because he will eat your dog.

As fierce as a tiger,
As cheeky as a monkey,
As strong as a boxer,
Very wet and stinky.

His name is Tangle Foot,
He lives in a bog,
Would you like to meet him?
Because he will eat your dog.

As evil as an alien,
As fast as a cheetah,

As scary as a lion,
He is a huge eater.

His name is Tangle Foot,
He lives in a bog,
Would you like to meet him?
Because he will eat your dog.

As fluffy as candyfloss,
As sneaky as a snake,
He is as tall as a bus
And he doesn't like to bake.

His name is Tangle Foot,
He lives in a bog,
Would you like to meet him?
Because he will eat your dog.

Jack Manion (9)
Low Furness CE Primary School, Great Urswick

Bay

Far, far away,
Where people come to stay,
There was a monster called Bay,
Even though he loves to play.

He's mean,
He's strong,
Even though,
He has a pong.

As tall as a human,
As mean as a man,
As silly as a pig,
As thick as a can.

He's mean,
He's strong,
Even though,
He has a pong.

"I just saw him!"
"Over there!"

Even though,
It was a bear.

He's mean,
He's strong,
Even though,
He has a pong.

He comes here,
At the dead of night,
To get some money,
For a kite.

He's mean,
He's strong,
Even though,
He has a pong.

But then he gets spotted
In daylight,
Then the cops come
To give him a fright.

He's mean,
He's strong,
Even though,
He has a pong.

Ben Hopkins (9)

Low Furness CE Primary School, Great Urswick

Rainboweyes

R ainboweyes is his name
A tiny tree is his home
I nside is magically huge
N o one is allowed in, only him
B ig is good for a big monster
O live is his second name
W indows open to let in the rain
E lectric flashing from his antlers
Y ou wouldn't believe it
E yes the colour of the rainbow
S even beautiful colours

He has a friend called Slimy
He lives in Rainbow Land
If you see him you'll get a fright
He makes lots of noise in the night.

Demi Elizabeth Garnett (9)
Low Furness CE Primary School, Great Urswick

Queenie's Rules!

There was a piece of fluff,
It was a little bit tough,
After it had been lying on the cold,
Wet, damp, street.

Inside the piece of fluff,
Was a small world,
Called Fluff Town,
All we knew was

The town hall was tiny,
Their world was always hot,
The monsters were even tinier,
As small as a full stop.

Their world was ruled by one,
Her name was Queenie,

Her eyes glowed like gold,
Her teeth amazingly sharp,
Her crown all shiny,
It even glowed in the dark!

The next day,
Everybody was fine,
It was like any other day,
All of a sudden

A dark cloud appeared,
Nobody knew what it was,
They thought a storm was coming,
But little did they know

It was really a human's foot!
They had no time.
Splat!
It was too late.

Kate C
Low Furness CE Primary School, Great Urswick

Piggle The Cheeky Monster

As hairy as a hamster,
As cheeky as a chimp,
Moody like Mr Wilson,
As fluffy as a rabbit,
Ears like horns,
Squeals like a pig.

Hilarious as a monkey,
As greedy as a hippo.
She was born in pickle town,
Loves candy,
Loud as an elephant,
As purple as a plum.

Horns like spikes,
As naughty as an elf,
As bouncy as beans,
Eyes like rat's teeth,
Smooth as a cat,
As cute as a puppy,
Hands like waffles.

Scary like a shark,
As slow as a snail,
As fat as a rat,
Mouth like the wind,
As big as a hill,
Has five hands and feet,
Likes pickles,
Does not like other people.

He lives on a rock,
He left his rock,
Went to Town.
His friend is Giggle,
Giggle did not like pickles,
Those two are a disaster.
Piggle only has pickles
In his house.

Faith Leigh Rhodes
Low Furness CE Primary School, Great Urswick

Tiny Tim's Poem

In a cold wet bin,
He was standing there,
The wind in his hair,
Whistling through the air.

The wind came,
The bin fell on its side
And it rolled down the hill
And something cried.

In a cold wet bin,
He was standing there,
The wind in his hair,
Whistling through the air.

He got out the bin
And he looked in a tin
For some food,
Then he crawled back in his bin.

In a cold wet bin,
He was standing there,

The wind in his hair,
Whistling through the air.

He was a stranger to people,
So they chucked cabbage at him
And radishes too
And they broke his bin.

In a cold wet bin,
He was standing there,
The wind in his hair,
Whistling through the air.

Frazier Brian Hazlehurst (9)
Low Furness CE Primary School, Great Urswick

Mamall's Party

One dark, stormy night,
Mamall couldn't fly his kite,
The weather was rough
And it was tough.

Mamall bean went to sleep,
His dream was kind of deep,
When Mamall woke up,
He had some bad luck.

Mamall bean had a party,
There was even a monster called Darty,
There were:
Dragon ones, short ones,
Pretty ones, scary ones,
Flying ones, stinky ones,
Naughty ones and invisible ones.

All of a sudden the cake went missing,
Then all the food and drink,
All of the guests started booing,
Then Mamall's face turned pink.

Mamall looked at Drake,
Drake had the lovely cake,
The cake had lost its shiny cherry,
But that didn't stop Mamall from being very merry.

Phoebe Day (8)
Low Furness CE Primary School, Great Urswick

The Tazer

As jumpy as a kangaroo,
As small as a mouse,
Teeth like swords,
Living in his big, black house.

Eyes like lava,
Feet like boats,
Made of emeralds,
Wearing his furry, green coat.

House made of coconuts,
You can come and stay,
Come and get a shock,
You will be sure to run away.

A long comes Frazier,
You don't want to meet him,
He might give you a taser,
If you dare!
They made a giant ship,
To destroy land,
To get green slime,
In the sand.

They visited Mars,
With a small ship,
They got golden bars,
To make a chip car.

They make a giant taser,
To destroy the world,
They set it off
And it destroyed the pearl.

Harvey Rhys Westwood (9)
Low Furness CE Primary School, Great Urswick

Reggie Is...

Reggie is
Naughty, sneaky, ambitious and scary,
Teeth like razors
And is really hairy.

But how did he get here?
Nobody knows.
Where does he live?
Nobody knows.

Reggie is
Naughty, sneaky, ambitious and scary,
Teeth like razors
And is really hairy.

As boring as literacy,
As cold as ice,
As sneaky as a snake.

Reggie is
Naughty, sneaky, ambitious and scary,
Teeth like razors
And is really hairy.

As smooth as a shark,
As creepy as a creeper,
As scary as a volcano,
And is a really big weeper.

Reggie is
Naughty, sneaky, ambitious and scary,
Teeth like razors
And is really hairy!

Ruby Enfys Fountain (9)
Low Furness CE Primary School, Great Urswick

Tibble Town

On a bright sunny day,
Monsters came to play,
One of them that came,
Dibble was his name.

People think they're scary
And some think they're hairy,
Dibble doesn't care
That he has lots of hair.

Dibble is a monster,
He has a friend called Bonster,
Bonster is his best friend,
They started off a new trend.

Dibble and Bonster were leaving,
The other monsters were seething,
Dibble and Bonster didn't care,
They just sat down on a chair.

They were bored of Tibble Town,
But didn't leave with a frown,

They knew it wasn't the end,
They'd go back to see their friends.

Orla S (8)
Low Furness CE Primary School, Great Urswick

The Fluffy Monster

He lives in a pocket,
His weapon is a socket.

What does he eat?
Nobody knows.

Is he good or bad?
Nobody knows.
He has razor sharp teeth,
Eyes like red fire,
As loud as a monkey,
He is very good at lying.

He lives in a pocket,
His weapon is a socket.

As crazy as Mrs Little,
As smelly as Mr Wilson.

He lives in a pocket,
His weapon is a socket.

His feet are like lava,
As red as can be,

That's why he's not friends with
You and me.

He lives in a pocket,
His weapon is a socket.

Toby (9)
Low Furness CE Primary School, Great Urswick

BlueBlar

I have a friend called BlueBlar,
He is blue and black,
He smells of parma violets.
He has very wavy arms.
He lives deep in outer space,
The planet BlueBlar, it is one of a kind.
BlueBlar can change his shape
And he has a forcefield around the planet,
He needs to change his shape to get off his planet.
BlueBlar is a fluffy, flying, fleabag!
He is most possibly the kindest alien ever.
He sees BlueBlar quite often.
His mum is called Scary Marey,
And his dad is called Scary Tarey.
He has two really good friends
Who are Cat in the Hat
And Rat with a Bat,
He is very short.

Florence Adams (8)
Low Furness CE Primary School, Great Urswick

Harold

Harold came from the past.
He is happy and hairy,
He makes people laugh with his funny jokes
And likes to play with his friends in the park.

He left the past to make people laugh
And tell them his funny jokes.
But he bumped into a mean, angry monster
Who said, "What are you laughing for?"
And bit him with his big jaws. Ouch!

Harold cried and sweets fell from his eyes,
The mean monster chewed the sweets.
Boom! Bang! Bam!
The mean monster turned red
And his jaws curled upwards.
He was smiling!

Rosie Lumb

Low Furness CE Primary School, Great Urswick

The Ptero-Snake

The ptero-snake lives in a fiery volcano,
In a deep, dark forest.
It smells like a rotten skeleton
With a wart on its eye.
On his snake body he has three eyes,
Four stitches and fourteen steamy spots.
He left the volcano in the deep dark forest,
To go and scare people with his sharp fangs.
He bit someone with his poisonous fangs
And they screamed, "Argh!"
The ptero-snake flew up in the air
And ate a blackbird.
He flew back down and ate limes.
He came face-to-face with a tiger.

Zach Parkinson (8)
Low Furness CE Primary School, Great Urswick

Hemmy

Hemmy lives in the deep, dark ocean,
Where she counts her seashells very often.
She smells like blueberry air freshener.
She left her home to collect,
Some dark and gloomy seashells.
While she was gone,
Some monster stole her seashells
That she had already collected.
She finished her journey and went home.
"My seashells have been stolen," she roared!
Bubbles flowed around her!
When the bubbles dissolved,
There in front of her was...
The biggest golden seashell ever.

Georgia Pip Sherrington (8)
Low Furness CE Primary School, Great Urswick

Bubble Pike

The Bubble Pike lives in the deep, dark tarn
And he has one eye bigger than the other.
He smells like seaweed
And likes to eat wiggly worms.
He left the tarn on an adventure to get food
But on the way, he found
Another Bubble Pike in the brambles,
Almost dead.
But Bubble Pike saved him from dying.
Bubble Pike waddled off looking for food.
The Bubble Pike who'd been rescued
Dived onto his hero,
They started fighting.
Boom! Bash!

Rohan Shaw
Low Furness CE Primary School, Great Urswick

Thanos

He has horns that burn
And teeth that shred like chainsaws,
His blood is as red as lava,
Nobody knows who he is.

Quick as an eagle,
Vicious as a Viking,
Cool as a coconut,
Cunning as a fox.

Where does he come from?
What does he eat?
Nobody knows,
Because he's a beast.

He only eats grass,
So you do not need to worry,
He comes from a cave,
Where nobody goes,
But still people do not know,
It is all a mystery.

Theo
Low Furness CE Primary School, Great Urswick

Boggle The Big Bad Bog Monster

His eyes yellow as a banana,
Dripping with mud dirt and leaves,
Claws like rat teeth,
Smelly as compost so don't dare breathe.

He hides away in a bog,
He never sees a frog,
He never sees a soul,
He hates to see a mole.

He wants to eat a frog,
He's as hungry as a hog,
The frog hops away,
Because he just wanted to play.

Grace Elizabeth Jewell (8)
Low Furness CE Primary School, Great Urswick

Fried Fred Your Chip-Eyed Friend

His head is red as his name is Fried Fred,
Covered with fur, with eyes made of fries,
Tongue is long, almost gone wrong,
He has stripes, brushed but rushed.
His home is the microwave, it's where he's from,
Can't you see this monster is cheeky number one?
Nobody can like him, they say he is an ugly fiend,
Judged by his cover, that's extremely mean,
If you bother to read, you'll see he's no evil demon,
He is eternally sad if he can't find
Another fry-eyed friend,
So join his search so he can be happy again.

Jake Carr (10)
North Lakes School, Penrith

This Thing!

This thing wakes me every morning,
Always yawning,
This thing wakes with a smile,
But it takes a while,
This thing is a gentle creature,
With friendly and loving features,
This thing is pink and fluffy like a marshmallow,
This thing is called Mellow.
She always says, "Hello!"
This thing has rainbow horns
And, when she thinks the day is done,
Then she has had all of her fun,
This thing goes to bed,
With a sleepy, sleepy head.

Ruby Gordon (10)
North Lakes School, Penrith

Lousious

Born on a farm.
Chomp! Chomp! Chomp!
Eating all the cake out of the bakery.
Chomp! Chomp! Chomp!
As loud as an earthquake.
Chomp! Chomp! Chomp!
Cute as a butterfly.
Chomp! Chomp! Chomp!
Popping all the footballs in sight.
Chomp! Chomp! Chomp!
Three friends she has.
Chomp! Chomp! Chomp!
One metre tall, like me.
Chomp! Chomp! Chomp!
It doesn't matter about height.

Crystal McGuinness (10)
North Lakes School, Penrith

Flum Bum Gum

F angs as sharp as knives,
L ikes to scare people's wives,
U nder the bed, he will creep,
M ostly when you sleep.

B ut, the only way to stop him is to turn him into mush,
U nfortunately, he hides in a very spiky bush,
M ay be friendly one day.

G reat, big claws, he roars on his way,
U nder the bed you slide,
M aybe you should hide.

Jay Whear (9)
North Lakes School, Penrith

Loverbug

"Shh!" went the trees,
"Don't wake our loverbug,
She's sleeping on high,
Resting her eyes."
Fluffy as a bear,
Gentle as can be,
Calm as the waves,
Splashing on the beach.
Sleeps in the mountains,
Hides at night,
Trying not to hurt,
Trying not to give a fright.
It once had friends,
But not any more,
Escaped to the Dark Woods,
To be by herself.

Gipsy Anne Scamp (10)
North Lakes School, Penrith

Bingo!

B eing the only monster in the USA,
I n England, he went to stay,
N o friends except rocks,
G ot really smelly socks,
O val and cute.

If I met him,
We could go to the gym,
We could get ice cream,
We'd be in a team,
He's funny and talented.

B ut he's got a toot,
O h Bingo,
Y es, it's me!

Eleonora Mitkus (10)
North Lakes School, Penrith

Rocket Boosters

There was once a monster called Mecfin,
He came from a space station and landed on
Earth.
Everyone was scared of him,
He just wanted to protect everyone,
No one wanted to be his friend.
Until, one day, someone came up to him,
They wanted to be his friend.
Mecfin accepted his request,
He was called Tom.
Mecfin finally had a friend,
They would be friends forever.

Oliver Lake (10)
North Lakes School, Penrith

Here Comes Jelly Belly!

Born in a jelly factory,
Wobble wobble, here comes Jelly Belly,
Wobble wobble, here comes Jelly Belly,
Shadowless, he floats along,
Like a snake, he bites you with his fangs,
Then you turn into a clone.
He is neon green,
With multicoloured patches on his body,
He has antennae that swing like aliens.

Alexis McGuinness (11)
North Lakes School, Penrith

Here Comes Jiggly Puff!

Boom! Boom! Boom!
Here comes Jiggly Puff with rainbow horns,
Giving hugs that nobody loves.
Boom! Boom! Boom!
Nails as sharp as the tip of an axe.
Boom! Boom! Boom!
Soft like a cloud with a rainbow touch.
Boom! Boom! Boom!
Next time, he will hug you too.

Simona Misiute (10)
North Lakes School, Penrith

The Lonely Monster

The lonely monster wails each night,
He wails and wails until the day is bright.
Everybody turns and runs,
When they hear the mighty monster hum.
When they hear the monster sing,
It makes everybody's ears ring.
He drives everyone round the bend,
If only he had a friend.

Sam Ramsay (9)
North Lakes School, Penrith

The Dragon's Breath

Dragon, dragon,
Under my bed.
Dragon, dragon,
Hiding in my shed.
Dragon, dragon,
Its eyes are red.
Dragon, dragon,
It needs to be fed.
Dragon, dragon,
Don't eat my head.
Dragon, dragon,
Get out of my head!

Claudiu Perdei (10)
North Lakes School, Penrith

Bobby!

B ig and evil mouth to chomp you up,
O ut of all the monsters, he's the most sensitive of them all,
B eing the only one in Scotland,
B eing the only one with a British accent,
Y es, that's me!

Mia Sedlak (9)

North Lakes School, Penrith

It's Grumpy The Monster

G ross and gruesome,
R ough and tough,
U gly and useless,
M enacing and moody,
P owerful and sleepy,
Y ellow and yucky.

Kai Sowerby (10)
North Lakes School, Penrith

Here Comes Mr Fang

F luffy and flying,
A ntennae and angry,
N aughty and noisy,
G iant with an evil mouth,
S tinky and sizzling with heat.

Byron Symes (10)
North Lakes School, Penrith

The Devil

Devil, Devil,
Eating my bed.
Devil, Devil,
In my shed.
Devil, Devil,
Its eyes are red.
Devil, Devil,
Stop following me!

Darius Pelin (10)
North Lakes School, Penrith

A Monster Horror

There was a monster,
As creepy as a zombie.
It was very bad,
It had no friends,
I don't know where it came from.

It had sharp claws and creepy paws,
Sabre-like teeth and bumpy, big horns,
Tentacle legs and a creepy head,
Sharp, clawed feet.
He had stitches and cuts,
One cat-like, green eye
And the other eyes were bright white,
With red veins inside.

Big veins pumped blood through his body
And leaked out of his mouth,
He had a rather big tummy,
Little, stubby hands.
But he could be more deadly.

It was really hard, but I did it,
At last, I killed the beast
And had a big feast.
But I still think another one's out there,
Lurking and waiting.

Jack Forsyth (9)
North Walney Primary School, Walney Island

The Ultimonster

The Ultimonster can inhabit anywhere in the world,
It can eat any meat,
But will sometimes eat plants for digestion.

Many people have tried to take it down,
But have found it bulletproof.
It is not a good creature
And has killed famous people.
It is out, still roaming the earth
And it can camouflage.
If you ever find this creature,
Run as fast as you can.

Godzilla is no longer the king of the monsters,
He has been dethroned by this creature!
I am the only person who can tame it,
This creature can see 100 miles in front of it.
And also, its roar can be heard from Syria!

James McQuistan (9)
North Walney Primary School, Walney Island

Monster Catastrophe

The monster is messy,
The monster is dirty
And the monster is long.
The monster has horns
Like red-hot chillis,
If you touch them,
You will burn with fear.
The monster has an eye,
Like a big blob of ink,
That drips onto his shirt
And stains the style of the shirt.
The monster has sturdy teeth
Like a scribble on a notebook.
The monster can carry
Heavy weights on his back,
As he walks along the path
The monster has red, burgundy skin
Like a flaming hot volcano.

Freya Grace Thomas (7)
North Walney Primary School, Walney Island

The Good Monster

I found a monster,
In a monster world
And the monster said,
"I am called Sally,
Can I be your friend?"

So, every month and day,
The purple spots shot out,
Bombs and fire.
It was good and sometimes naughty.

I saw a small monster,
It was called Mike,
It had one eye.

Mike and Sally ate
Rubbish and flowers,
They were best friends.

Amy Hunt (9)
North Walney Primary School, Walney Island

Roller Girl

Pink and quick, kind and fast,
Zooming around like a black cat,
Where she lives is an awesome land,
Long haired with pink bows in her hair.
Rollerblades so she can zoom around
With happiness, everywhere.
She is friends with Mr Goatie and Candy Girl,
Ripped jeans with a belly top,
One eye and multicoloured bobbles.

Esme Hambleton (8)
North Walney Primary School, Walney Island

Cuddle Team Leader

As I was in the woods,
I saw the neighbourhood.

There was a monster with a rainbow tail
And I also saw a snail.

She had beautiful eyes
And she was really shy.

She had a colourful horn,
She slept on a thorn.

She came with me to KFC
And I lost my key.

We ate with the queen,
We saw someone clean.

Then we saw a fool,
In our pool.

We played at the park,
She had a big bark.

Then we went home,
We said hello to the gnome.

Dakota Ayanna Fulton (8)
Northside Primary School, Northside

Guzzlin Day!

Greed is wicked, basic and vile,
But once a year, it makes us smile,
So bust a gut at our buffet
And stuff your face on Guzzlin Day!

Self control's for lesser folk,
So pack your gob until you choke,
Cram your maw, eat like thunder,
Gobble down until you chunder.

Gluttons rule for one day only,
Wolf down a horse, pig out on pony,
Cows' foot pie, goats' head soup,
Fill your boots until you poop.

Give your guts another beating,
When you're stuffed don't stop eating,
Guzzle up til you're unable,
If you can stand, don't leave the table!

Amy-Lee Summer Harris (9)
Ormsgill Nursery & Primary School, Barrow-In-Furness

Monster Woman

The Monster Woman is as tall
As a double-decker bus,
She eats children, grass, mud and pus.
She has one big, wonky eye
And it's filled with corned beef pie.
She lives in a stinky pond
And trades it for a magic wand.
Her scaly, long arms are as crusty as her palms,
She has four legs and four arms.

Keira Nelson (10)
Ormsgill Nursery & Primary School, Barrow-In-Furness

Danny, The Death Machine

Danny is really lethal,
When he drools, he feels griefful.
He has four hands
And he likes to live in many lands.
He has two ears
And never fears.
He eats cats,
But he likes them more
When sitting on mats.
Danny is about nine foot nine,
And he has a hobby of crime.

Rya Bentley (11)
Ormsgill Nursery & Primary School, Barrow-In-Furness

The Shape-Shifters

Grendell is a selfish and horrifying beast,
On your body, he will feast
Like a monstrous beast.
He is a miserable beast.
Filled with eyeballs in his intestines,
He will feed on your head,
He's very keen and he is mean.

Keelan Lee Purcell (10)
Ormsgill Nursery & Primary School, Barrow-In-Furness

The Poem Of Slenderrina

Slenderrina has snake-like eyes
She will pounce on you and give you a surprise
She has an extremely sharp, dagger-like tail
Her skin is so scaly and pale.

Yazmin Martin (10)
Ormsgill Nursery & Primary School, Barrow-In-Furness

Demon Slayer

Let me introduce the Demon Slayer.
He had teeth like daggers
And he was a gross spitter,
His eyes were evil,
The Devil couldn't be badder.

His was as vicious as a crocodile,
He didn't realise as he was in denial,
Angrily stomping without style,
Fiercy figthing all the while.
He headed to a city, disguised,
Realising that he would be recognised.

The burning glow in his eyes,
The city was resilient, except for fearful cries.

Stomping loudly behind the rain,
Getting soaked by the rain,
Leaving bloodstains.
The army came in a gigantic tank,
But everything went blank,
He escaped the city and ate a kitty,
He stayed in the countryside because it was pretty.

Jamie Swanton (8)
St Thomas CE Primary School, Kendal

The Monster

There was a king that was nowhere near glorious,
Because there was a monster that was dangerous
And his muscles were terribly monstrous,
With this monster, the broken city was never
momentous.

He killed all the humans and ate all their dairy,
He really was big, the opposite of a fairy,
On the inside, he was so hairy,
People ran away from him
Because he was so scary.

He was not adopted, he didn't have a home,
His hair was a terrible mess, he hadn't got a comb,
His heart was horrible, the size of a dome,
His eyes were squishy, they felt like foam.

For his dinner, he had a lobster
You'd think you were the strongest, he is stronger.
He was never on stage, but he was a songster.
In the city, he was a destroyer.

He used to smack people,
He gave them a good whip,
He had a move called The Rip.
He had lots of bones and blood as a dip,
He used to squeeze them with his good grip.

He would take all their things, he'd always rob,
He showed no mercy, he would never stop,
He never obeyed anyone, he didn't have a job,
I hope you will believe that he was in a mob.

He was so powerful, he could jump to the moon,
He was so heavy, the opposite of a balloon,
He was so strong, he could snap a spoon,
I hoped he would be killed soon.

When he was nervous, his eyes would squint,
He was so fast, he had to sprint,
When he ran, he left a big footprint.
Where was his footprint? I'll give you a hint.

Thomas Perruzza (9)
St Thomas CE Primary School, Kendal

Wingerbell

There was a monster called Wingerbell,
He liked to yell and he did smell.
When you were around him,
It was like you were in hell.
His wings were red and
The rest was the colour of a bluebell.

He acted very devilish and tricksy,
There he was, acting like a pixie,
His attitude was weird, it was mixed,
He had a secret crush on a monster called Cherry.

Wingerbell went on a journey to impress her,
He wrote a love book and became an author,
All the girls loved him and began to purr,
But all he saw of them was a blur.

Cherry looked like a fish,
But Wingerbell thought she was a dish,
Wingerbell made a wish,
That they would go on a date, it would be swish.

He got lost and thought of Cherry,
And then he started to feel merry,
So Wingerbell travelled back,
Because he thought it was necessary.
He asked someone for directions, called Carry.

Wingerbell got back, Cherry had a boyfriend,
He felt sad and his heart needed to mend,
So he went to the shop to get into a trend.
A few days later, their relationship was a dead end.

He then went out with a lady called Dove,
They were deeply in love,
Then Dove started to shove,
With a jelly bean glove.

Wingerbell broke up with Dove,
Now he was with Cherry,
They got married, feeling merry.
With their love, they were quite weary,
They were happy and lived in a berry.

Talitha Rushton (9)
St Thomas CE Primary School, Kendal

Squdevry

Let me introduce Squdevry.
He never gave off any energy,
With terrifying teeth
And was hairy on his underneath.

He was always in a foul mood
And sweet baked beings are his food.
When he is sleeping
He dreams of all things bad,
He was horrendous and gobbles people up
When he is mad.

But there was a wedding in the city,
He never liked them, what a pity.
He sneaked down to the wedding
Cleverly dressed in some bedding.

He went there with a helicopter jet-pack
And in his hands were a sword and a sack.
When he got there, he chased the groom
And stomped on the bride's flowers
From Blossom Bloom.

The police came, someone must have called.
Squdevry was surprised and appalled.
He ran away to a nearby cave
And found a man, who made him work as his slave.

The old man's rules were very tame,
Squdevry thought the man would die in shame.
But the next day, he heard
The marriage was going again.
"Ouch!" Squdevry exclaimed,
"My head really hurts with pain."

"I hate marriages, they are foul.
I need to wipe my sweat now, give me a towel!
I hate this place and you, little man."
And he ran out of the cave with
A fish and a frying pan.

When he got to his cosy bed,
He turned off the lights and decided instead
That the first thing he would do
Was kill me and you.

Annabel Towler (9)
St Thomas CE Primary School, Kendal

The Story Of Spiral Wing

Let me introduce Spiral Wing,
An outrageous monster,
Who liked to eat raw lobster.
She was annoying and has a huge amount of fur
She ran around frantically, she was a bit of a blur.

She was a bit of a show-off and didn't care,
She had lots of nits in her hair.
She got on a bus with a weird driver,
She got to the train station
And saw the Pied Piper.

She took a train to London,
And looked around a dungeon,
She met a boy called Brendan,
Who took her to the Tower of London.

The monster was in love with Brendan,
She went to see the Tower's dungeon,
She felt magical, splendid and lovely too,
Brendan exclaimed that he needed the loo.

The monster was all alone in the prison,
She really missed Brendan,
So she carried on up the Tower of London.
She saw the crown and wanted it,
She waited for Brendan.

"Brendan, you're back," she cried.
"Do you want to go on the Tower ride?"
They went on the ride with lots of pride
And Brendan nearly died.

She went back to the Tower,
To get in, she used all her power.
Then, when she got the crown she had a shower.
In the shower, she went, "Girl power!"

Just then, off went the burglar alarm,
Good thing she had her lucky charm.
Then the guardsman came and got her arm,
When she went to jail, it smelled like a farm.

Molly-May Holleran (9)
St Thomas CE Primary School, Kendal

The Little Monster

Let me introduce a monster called Fuzzy,
She loved crumble, especially blackberry.
She teleported herself to Monster High,
While she was there, she ate lots of pie.

The next day, she met a friend called Spiky,
They did lots of pranks that were very cheeky
And accidentally went to the human world,
But Spiky said, "Do three twirls!"

Once they did three twirls, they separated
And suddenly evaporated.
She went to see her family
And found out her mom worked at a bakery.

Through the weeks, she went
To go on an adventure,
They always went together to get surprises.
They were always different shapes and sizes.

The challenge was to save the princess,
To get her, they needed to go
Over the lava bridges,

They loved challenges
And going to places...

At last it was time to state the winner
And it was chicken dinner.
Spiky and Fuzzy said, "Yum!
That is definitely going in my tum!"

The winner was Spiky and Fuzzy, those two girls,
She forgot to tell them the other surprise
Was a box of pearls.
"I love pearls!" said Fuzzy.
"I am so happy, what I am feeling inside is funny."

After they went to Fuzzy's family,
Everyone was so happy,
They cheered with laughter
And lived hapily, ever after.

Florrie Stalker (8)
St Thomas CE Primary School, Kendal

My Monster's Journey

Have you heard of a monster, who's such a dude
And his attitude is cheeky and rude?
He's always in a jokey mood
And walks around half-nude.

He has lots of girls,
Which are geniune pearls
And he asks them to do twirls
And all the girls have curls.

One day, he went on a big trip,
With his very useful whip,
Held with all his mighty grip,
Getting hungry, he licked his lip.

Then a pack of wolves suddenly attacked.
The monster said, "What a lovely snack."
A fierce wolf jumped on his back,
The monster got angry and, *thwack!*

He stumbled into a desert, sore and bleeding,
So much help was he needing.

A big, fat monkey was misleading,
The monkey thought he was feeding.

Then, with all his might,
He punched the monkey in the head,
It fell to the ground as his head bled.
It took a while for the monster to see it was dead,
The monkey's blood was bright red.

Then he picked up the monkey with all his strength
And then had to walk a great length,
He was counting his miles, he was on the tenth,
He bellowed, which made a wavelength.

The monster brought it to the king,
"I didn't want a monkey, you stupid thing."
The king's temper was really raging,
He decided to banish him to Beijing.

Joseph William Green (8)
St Thomas CE Primary School, Kendal

The Aggressive Fluffball

Let me tell you about a vile, fierce, little monster
Who lived behind a door,
That people wished to tear and tear
And my monster had a gigantic jaw.

Fluffballs were very careless
And they made a huge, sticky mess,
Don't call them a big, cheeky pest,
Or you'll need a rest.

My monster lived in the cellar,
Of the ancient shop called Shella.
This creature is called Fuzzbella,
Her favourite thing was Nutella.

Ellie was a silly girl.
"Beware of danger," said her Uncle Twirl.
"Their razor teeth are as white as a pearl,
Just thinking about it makes me curl."

In the middle of the night,
Ellie was ready to have a fight.

She crept up to Shell with all her might
And turned on the light, which was very bright.

She shouted, "Come out you fuzzball!"
Ellie felt that, in any second, she would fall.
She got dragged into a hall,
That looked like a large mall.

Then Fuzzbella took off Ellie's trouser ants,
That looked like the flag from France.
And in the pockets were lots of pants,
This was Ellie's last chance.

In the morning, she sprinted quickly, screaming,
Ellie's mum and dad were fuming.
Fuzzbella was happily looming,
But the tiny village was crying.

Norah Murray (8)
St Thomas CE Primary School, Kendal

Spiky

Let me introduce you to a monster called Spiky,
Spiky was sweet like honey.
Spiky was a bunny,
She would be an amazing bunny,
She acted like a monkey.

She was never a careless person to me,
When she went in water,
It felt like a sting from a bee.
She was the carer of the sea,
I never took fluff for free.

She was a wonderful, fuzzy ball,
Spiky loved playing with dolls,
She would never prank call,
Spiky loved being in France.

She loved her home, Monster High,
She could teleport to Monster High.
She loved to go high while she flew,
Spiky was a little bit shy.

There was a challenge to save the princess,
They worked together to win the surprises,
That were all different shapes and sizes.

She loved to play games,
She didn't care what name,
She never claimed something
That wasn't hers to claim,
She loved to be in frames.

Spiky would never turn her back on me,
We got the key and saw the princess.
There were lava bricks,
We had to cross three.
We always loved pies for tea.

After a year, Spiky went back
To her parents for the last time,
She went back to her friends to make slime.
She liked to climb,
My friend would always give me
Something that was mine.

Layla Goodyear (9)
St Thomas CE Primary School, Kendal

Baitlin

Let me introduce Baitlin,
Her best friend was the amazing Caitlin,
She hated her banana medicine,
She put her dinner in the bin,
She wanted to begin
And she had a vitamin.

The only reason she was famous,
She always looked and felt glamorous,
It's because she was so dangerous,
She was always mischievous,
She was always horrendous,
Her breath was so poisonous.

Until, one day, a prince arrived,
He smelled like chives,
He gave her high-fives,
Baitlin thought he would have a lot of wives.

Baitlin was lovely when the prince arrives,
She put on her perfume that smelled like chives,
The prince thought she was a lovely monster,
I don't know how she was alive.

She liked every city,
I don't know why, but she was so sassy,
She acted friendly,
It was such a pity.

The monster and the prince fell in love,
They bought some doves,
They loved to wear gloves,
They were like a sparkly heart of love.

But she went home with Furbie, not the prince,
They haven't seen each other since,
I didn't know why, because he had a good rinse,
They needed to convince,
The monster and Furbie to love the prince.

Caitlin Suzanne Whittaker (8)
St Thomas CE Primary School, Kendal

Pennywise The Hungry Monster

There was once a monster called Pennywise,
Every day, he would never apologise,
Good guys were what he would despise,
He always wanted to win a prize.

He went on a journey to find some blood
And tripped over and face-planted in the mud,
Now he wanted to eat a jacket spud,
Next, he made a massive flood.

He went to America
And ate pigs from Costa Rica,
He also ate someone called Erika,
Then he called America Cherrica.

He ate cows and sheep in Kendal
And someone called Lendall,
He felt really ungentle,
Well, he was very mental.

He killed three horses and sheep in Windermere,
"Oh my goodness," he said, "the river is near."
Pennywise ate a girl called Leah,
Then next day, the winter got near.

He killed five humans and went for a swim,
Then he went to lose weight at the gym,
Two minutes later, he saw his friend, Tim,
And they both sang a monster hymn.

He killed a deer and two pigs
And met a boy called Briggs,
Briggs ate some twigs,
Pennywise ate more pigs.

Pennywise drowned,
Near all the clowns,
Who were practising touch-downs
And some were practising their nouns.

Skye Atkinson (8)
St Thomas CE Primary School, Kendal

The Monster

Let me introduce a super, furry monster,
Its name is Kipper, a real prankster,
Such a gangster, buying a hamster
And he always knows the right answer.

A grumpy mood is why he was so famous,
It loved to be blameless,
Sleep is when it dreamed of all things dangerous,
Awful thoughts that were horrendous.

Kipper wanted a wife who was super lonely,
He felt really comfy, cuddly and snuggly,
No longer really ugly, but sweet like honey,
He knew what to do, he had to rescue Fluffy.

Up and down the street,
In a flashing heartbeat,
Up the long high street,
Down the short, grubby street.

It was quite dismal and dark,
Inside the dismal park,

There wasn't even a flashing spark,
Kipper needed to find the bad-behaved clerk.

The clock house was super bright,
The guards put up a fabulous fight,
But Kipper had a lot of might,
He held Fluffy super tight.

They ran back,
It was quite dark and black,
Kipper couldn't wait for a snack,
They were going off track.

He travelled back home,
They had conquered Rome,
Fluffy was as sweet as honeycomb,
Kipper fell asleep in foam.

Nicole Fiderewicz (9)
St Thomas CE Primary School, Kendal

The Cool Demon

Let me introduce, Cool Demon monster,
He eats like a lion, what a monster,
Humans and deer are what he will slaughter,
If you enter his cave, he'll kill the imposter.

This demon is frightening,
Just like lightning,
The winged thing from the lord king,
Just hated cycling.

He travelled to Japan,
And ate some eggs and ham,
Then rammed a pram,
He also slipped on jam.

He always does lots of farts,
And nearly got shot by darts,
His butt-mobile is his cart,
He really hates art.

He scares everyone to death,
And nearly puts them out of breath,

He met someone called Beth,
And put her to death.

The villagers bought a machine gun,
That shot up high, as high as the sun,
The egg that came out spun,
Glory! The villagers had won!

Boom! Cool Demon was knocked out,
Oh my goodness, there was no doubt,
One of the villagers ate a sprout,
Cool Demon was still knocked out.

He woke up in a zoo,
And didn't know what to do,
Then he got through, into the loo,
And he had a great number two.

Chris Russel (9)
St Thomas CE Primary School, Kendal

My Monster's Dream Holiday

Let me introduce you to a monster
That is a real conker.
He runs faster than a cheetah
And he is a real adder.
His skin is very colourful, but mostly amber.

He wished to go on holiday
Where there's loads of snow
Because, when he was covered in it,
He started to glow.
On his dream holiday, he met a girl called Jo
And, as soon as he met her,
He saw her beautiful bow.

In a hall, they sat at a table.
A waiter came over and said
That her name was Mable.
When her wobbly legs were stable,
She read out the food from a label.
When she walked away, she tripped on a cable.

That night, they watched Romeo and Juliet.
The monster thought,
DId they meet on the internet?

The next day they went skiing
And fell off a cliff.
The monster caught her
With a hand that was very stiff.
Jo thanked him with a big, sloppy kiss.
Once she'd finished, she fell into the mist.

The monster was heart-broken,
His love was lost,
His mind went criss-crossed.
He walked off through the frost.

Seb Cox (8)
St Thomas CE Primary School, Kendal

Boxer

Let me introduce my ugly monster,
My monster is called Boxer.
Boxer eats like a lobster,
Boxer is a caring monster.

Boxer likes to sleep,
He likes to leap,
Boxer likes to get things cheap,
He should be counting sheep.

He stomped angrily to work with his friend Mark,
When he finished, it was dark,
He saw a sparkly dog and it said, "Bark!"
Boxer rolled clumsily to the park.

He saw something lovely,
Boxer felt bubbly, fuzzy and comfy.
Boxer liked to eat honey,
It was really runny.

He went on skiis down a mountain.
At night, Boxer loved counting.

I loved bouncing,
My dog liked howling.

In the corner of his eye,
He saw a rat
And sat on a mat
And he wore a hat.

Boxer went shopping,
So he could do some mopping,
He bought a TV for some watching,
On the way back home, he started hopping.

When he got home, he unpacked the bags,
And he found a lucky flag,
Then he went to Mars and played tag
And he went nag, nag, nag.

Amy Fiderewicz (9)
St Thomas CE Primary School, Kendal

Bendy The Poem

Let me introduce a monster called Bendy
And he was quite trendy,
He hated people called Wendy
And he wasn't that friendly.

Bendy had four arms
And he loved food from farms
And he caused such bad harm,
He wanted another arm.

He met a girl called Molly,
Who looked like a dolly
And she was so jolly,
She walked around with her brolly.

He met his friend called Jay
And his birthday was in May
And he sat next to the bay,
With his other friend called Pey.

He started to fly,
And he shouted goodbye,

So he started to cry
And then he got all shy.

He liked to kick,
With his best friend Mick
And he loved to eat some chocolate biscuits,
Whilst taking lots of pics.

They went on a ride
And then lied,
So they got pied
And then they all cried.

They went in a tower
And they all got a power,
So they had a shower
And they took an hour.

Keisha Miller (9)
St Thomas CE Primary School, Kendal

Jake

There once was a terrible monster named Jake,
Who stuffed his chubby face with cake,
Whilst sitting by a lake.
He once went to Turkey,
Where all the water was murky.

The weather was boiling and sunny,
But everyone thought he walked funny,
With his warts and his boils, he looked fearsome,
He gnawed things that looked awesome.

Everyone scattered when he limped off the plane,
Which upset the famous man, Dwayne.
When he skipped on the beach,
He swallowed a leech.

When he went to check in,
He tumbled into a bin.
When he went to the pool,
Everyone thought he was a fool.

When he trotted to dinner,
There was a club and he was a beginner.

If he didn't get his food,
He would be in a bad mood.

When he came back,
He travelled on a muddy track,
After his journey, he had a snack
And he saw a duck go quack.

Jackson Barber (9)
St Thomas CE Primary School, Kendal

Cool Bubnub

Let me introduce a lovely monster,
Its name was Bubnub, a proper gangster,
And he was a massive banger,
'Cause he was an exciting swimmer.

He was powerful and colourful,
But he was excitable
And so clever,
Like an educated man.

He swam for metres
And came with a beater.
But he was a cheater
And he still won with that healthy body.
So he celebrated.

Then he got a massive surprise
And it was a monkey,
Who was a bit chunky,
But so funky!

So he was happy,
But a bit flappy

And felt ugly,
'Cause he turned badly.

So he killed everyone
And got bold,
'Cause he was told,
To be careful.

Jay Grattan (9)
St Thomas CE Primary School, Kendal

Destroya

That was my monster, he was called Destroya.
He was fiercely fierce with his ears pierced
And he went on a hunt with a little grunt.

He found a little thing
And destroyed it with his head
And then he went to bed.
He also went to destroy the city,
What a pity. And he found a piggy,
His name was Ziggy.

Ziggy threw him away to a far away place
That was full of zombies,
It wasn't very pretty.
He attacked quickly,
Zombies were dying,
Which wasn't a pity.

Destroya eventually won the victory royale,
Everyone was pleased, they called him a pal.

Jenson Jay Hawad (8)
St Thomas CE Primary School, Kendal

Jack, The Scared Monster

Jack is my monster, he's always in a cage,
Because he was scared to go to the village,
One day, arrived a huge partridge,
Which was full of delicious porridge.

He swallowed it quickly,
His gigantic teeth looked so prickly,
Everyone screamed and ran away speedily.

Jack began to feed and not behave,
So he stomped out of his cave
And killed everyone with a shockwave.

Jack stacked up a humongous five laser beam
But then he was cross,
He thought it was very mean.
Then he cleaned the mess,
So he decided to make everything clean.

Aimee Louise Taylor (9)
St Thomas CE Primary School, Kendal

YOUNG WRITERS INFORMATION

We hope you have enjoyed reading this book – and that you will continue to in the coming years.

If you're a young writer who enjoys reading and creative writing, or the parent of an enthusiastic poet or story writer, do visit our website **www.youngwriters.co.uk**. Here you will find free competitions, workshops and games, as well as recommended reads, a poetry glossary and our blog.

If you would like to order further copies of this book, or any of our other titles, then please give us a call or visit **www.youngwriters.co.uk**.

Young Writers
Remus House
Coltsfoot Drive
Peterborough
PE2 9BF
(01733) 890066
info@youngwriters.co.uk